ABYSS

Thought provoking poetry & prose

D.G. TORRENS

Copyright © 2018 D.G. TORRENS
All rights reserved.
ABYSS
Edition 1.

This is a work of fiction. Names, characters, businesses, places, events and incidents either are the products of the author's imagination or used in a fictitious manner. Any resemblance to actual persons, living or dead, or actual events is purely coincidental.

License Notes: This Book is licensed for your personal enjoyment only. This Book may not be re-sold or given away to other people. If you would like to share this book with another person, please purchase an additional copy for each person you share it with.

If you are reading this book and did not purchase it, or it was not purchased for your use only, then you should return to Amazon.com and purchase your own copy. Thank you for respecting the hard work of this author.
All rights reserved. No part of this book may be reproduced, stored in a retrieval system or transmitted in any form or by any means without the prior written permission of the author

Cover design by D.G. Torrens
Formatting by Damo Jackson

All images used in this publication sourced CCO free for public domain use.

ISBN-10: 1984145193
ISBN-13: 978-1984145192

I have come to understand the darkness and respect the times we are forced to share -

-TITLES-

Biographies & Memoirs
Amelia's Story

Amelia's Destiny

Amelia the Mother

Contemporary & Military Romance
Broken Wings

Tears of Endurance (Ferria/Fielding Novel)

Whispers from Heaven (Ferria/Fielding Novel)

The Poppy Fields (Book 1)

The Poppy Fields (Book 2)

The Poppy Field (Book 3)

A Soldier's Fear

Romantic Suspense
Forbidden (Hamilton/Sharma Novel)

Dissolution (Hamilton/Sharma novel)

Finding You

Amnesia

One For Sorrow

Poetry
Military Boots

From the Author

Poetry is a unique voice that can deliver words to people in ways normal conversation cannot. The words resonate and make you think. The words can be like sutures, healing from the inside out.

Someone finally gets you and you are not alone. The words make sense and you realise that maybe I am not going crazy after all. You conclude, it is not just me; I am not alone in my darkness...

ABYSS takes the reader on a journey – a journey we are all forced to take at some point in our lives. When we are suffering inwardly, we often keep our inner suffering concealed from those closest to us. We put on a brave face and smile when all we want to do is cry and scream aloud. Winning the fight is not easy. The fight can feel like an endless battle and consume you from the inside out.

The dark shadows buried deep in the far corners of our minds when we are at our most vulnerable, feed on our pain – loss, grief, rejection, depression, anxiety and much more. No one is immune.

Through the art of poetry, I have touched on these raw emotions. I have delved deep into the darkness that I have journeyed in my lifetime to convey the emotional struggles that I know plague many. Emotional struggles are not a human defect – it's naturally human.

D.G. Torrens –

Chapter One

JOURNEYING THE ABYSS

Abyss

Skulking in the shadows of my mind

Waiting patiently like a panther
Ready to assail its prey

My nemesis – an ineffable fault line
I can feel the force of it

Breathing down my neck
Invisible but ever present

My will is strong – I continue to fight
Ensuring a distance between my nemesis and me.

Unseen Chains - Prisoner

I open my eyes and allow them to adjust
In that brief moment, I was free –
Until
Reality awakens me
CHAINED
Imprisoned once more
I try to rise from my slumber
My body holds me hostage
CHAINED
I turn over
My will has taken leave
For now at least
CHAINED –
I am to weakened to fight
I am alive yet between worlds
I try again to rise from my slumber
CHAINED
Imprisoned no freedom insight
Snap out of it, I hear you say
Your words are lost on me
CHAINED
I hide behind a shield
One with a smile for the world
I have no option but to rise
CHAINED
Invisible to all those around me
For only I see my chains
My abyss has swallowed me whole

CHAINED

I open my eyes and allow them to adjust
Today is different for I am free
Released from my chains
For now at least.

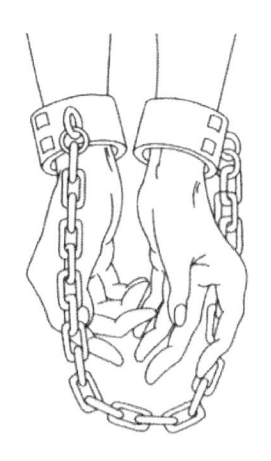

Don't Accept My Words

Do you hear my cry?
The one buried deep in my voice
Look into my eyes
And you will see my pain –
I smile
I tell you I am fine
But I am swallowed up in despair

I want to scream
But my voice is silenced
Silenced by the fear of judgemental ears

Look into my eyes
Do not accept my words
My pain is shielded
I need to talk
But I am afraid

My voice is silenced
I want to scream

Look into my eyes
My pain buried deep behind them
Do not accept my words
and walk away
I need you.

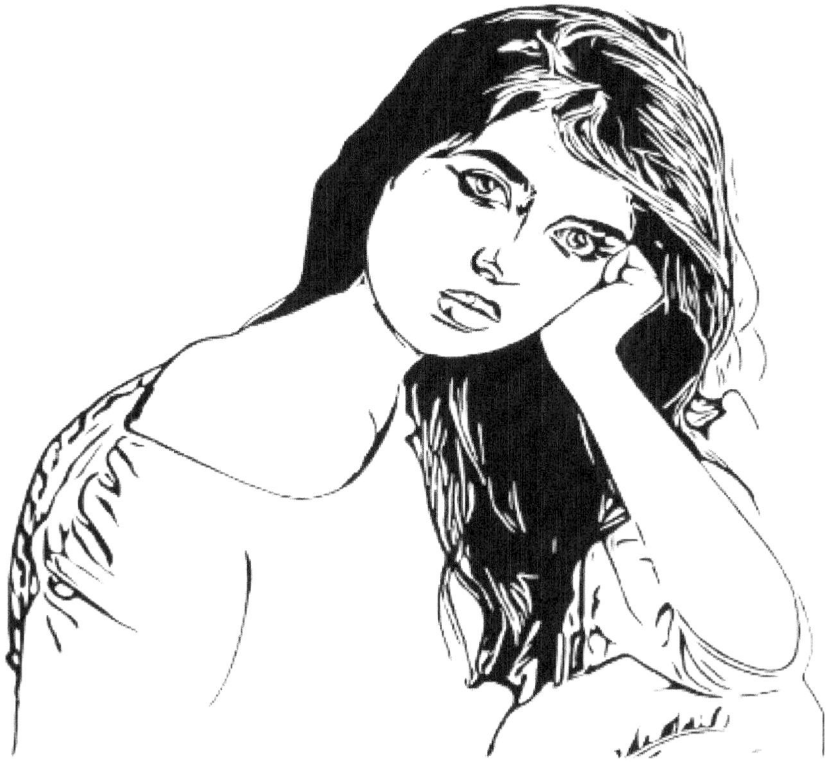

Hidden Emotions

A plethora of emotions consume my soul
A fixed smile on my face for the world

    While a war is emerging inside of me
    A war of conflicted emotions –
    A battle that cannot be won

        'How are you today?' I am asked
        'I'm fine thank you,' is my reply.

Abyss -

A perpetual dark hole we shall all journey if only for a moment –

— D.G. TORRENS

Not Worthy

You told me so often
I was not worthy
You told me so often
I will amount to nothing
Your words tattooed to my heart
A constant reminder –
Of what you believed
I could never be
You told me so often
I was not worthy
That I believed you were right
I was not worthy
I would amount to nothing
You told me so often
There was no place for me
No one would love me
I was not worthy
And for so long
I believed you.

Lost

I lost me
I am on the outside
Looking in
Lost deep
In a perpetual loop
Grasping for my sanity

                    Held only by an
                    Invisible thread

                                      Fragile and wanting
                                        To find me again.

Pressure

Sometimes, the pressure is too much

        Sometimes, I don't want to be responsible

Sometimes, I just want to be –

        Not what you want me to be

Sometimes, I don't want to be what I am supposed to be –

        Sometimes, I just want to be what I want to be

Sometimes, the pressure is just too much.

You Left Me Mourning

I am in mourning
Yet you live
The pain unbearable
My heart in shreds
No longer mine
You took your leave
Your heart
Your love
You left me mourning
It is worse than death
For I live it over and over
I gifted you my heart
My love
My everything
And you threw it away
In that moment -
I knew
I would never love again.

Archenemy

I stared into my Abyss
A black hole of
Nothingness
Stared right back
A familiar feeling
My archenemy
One that I had
Come to respect
I drew my sword
Corrected my stance
But my eyes don't see
You overpowered me
Slain to the ground
You won this battle
But not the fight
I will be ready
Next time we fight.

I woke up today

I took my first breath

and stepped out of bed

today is a good day –

— D.G. TORRENS

Betrayed Heart

A pained heart
Feels every arrow
Filled with holes
In tatters

        I knew -
        I knew for a while
        Hanging on with all my being
        Your love has transferred

                And still –
                I whisper I love you
                Silence ensues
                Your pause betrays you

        You step out of bed
        Averting my gaze
        'I'm sorry'
        You whisper

Then leave for the last time
A pained heart feels every arrow
Filled with holes
In tatters.

A Butchered Heart

You cut open my heart
You held it – beating

                In that moment
                The beating stopped

                                Your cold hands
                                Splintered my heart

              No suture offered
              Silence ensued
              As I watched you walk away.

Closed Heart

In that moment

I knew –

I would never feel

Love again.

Pain is a process we

have to see through –

— D.G. TORRENS

Spoken

Your silence is deafening
Enshrouding my space
I can hear your words
Your silence has spoken

                I extend my arm
              Reaching out to you
                Amidst this space
                  I feel nothing

                                I hear your cries
                          Your silence has spoken
                                Then I remember
                        I LAY THEE TO REST –

Bitter Tongue

Lay your bitter tongue to rest

        For it casts venom unlike no other

                Offer instead a suture for the many
                          Pained hearts

      Know that your words slain like a sword
      Wielded with your accompanied smile

You do not deserve the gift of speech
The most powerful gift of all.

Your Gift

You gifted me your vulnerability
The purest part of you – revealing all that you are

                I am intoxicated by your truths
                My heart now overwhelmed

There is sublime beauty in your candour
Displayed before me like a Picasso

                I do not look on with confusion
                I see you now with great clarity.

Clothed in Decaying Flesh

Clothed in decaying flesh
Humanity's reality
Dress it how you like –
This will never change
Hiding the floors of our existence

        Has become our obsession
        Yet the beauty lies in the reality
        Not in the camouflage
        I revel in God's humour
        For he has the last laugh.

Mendacious Minds

Mendacious people know nothing of truth

        They skulk in the shadows –
        Assessing their prey

                Innocent victims
                Blinded

      Blinded by their own kind hearts
    Their lives seared by a poison arrow of words
Untruths fragmenting everything they thought to be true.

Shape-Shifter

You are a shape-shifter changing form without warning
The words trip off your tongue with ease
Words that mean nothing to you
Yet mean everything to me
The power you have over my heart
Is crushing me
Yet I cannot break free
You are my addiction
A habit I cannot break
Unpredictable in nature
Unpredictable in love
You continually weaken my resolve
But I am getting stronger by the day
One day, I will be gone
One day
You will lose the only person
That loved you more than you love yourself.

Anxiety

Nervous
Her hands slip under the table
Where they cannot be seen
She pings the band
Secured around her wrist
The pinch on her skin
A momentary burn
Anxiety released
For this moment
At least.

Humankind-Our Worst Enemy

Our world no longer makes sense to me
Compassion eludes the masses
Our filter of kindness buried in a perpetual abyss
Cruel is ruling and many suffer
I sense an apocalyptic cloud is ready
To unleash its contents
Blinded and deafened we step forward –
Controlled by our own ignorance
The signs are clear
Yet we do not see
Still, we step forward eyes wide shut
No accountability
Only irreversible destruction
Humankind – our worst enemy.

The past broke me and my journey forward healed me.

I peeked through the fabric of my reality and this changed the way I viewed my world –

— D.G. TORRENS

Caged in Time

I miss your breath whispering to my
neck your hands entwined in mine

        I miss your eyes enveloping my soul
          Telling me all I need to hear

                I long for those moments
                I was locked in your arms

    Moments when time ceased to exist
    Now I'm a hostage to memories stored
    Caged in a time that no longer exists.

Broken Heart

When all around you is falling apart
The world is turning regardless

    You are crying for your weeping heart
    That suffers daily in the darkness

        Your spirit is lost; your spirit beaten
        Hiding in a world that could not care less

    A broken heart and a will that's weakened
    The world keeps turning regardless.

Loneliness

Loneliness is a hurting feeling
I wish I could explain
It comes at you from nowhere
And plagues your soul with pain

        I extend my arm and reach for you
        Then look into your eyes
        You turn and walk away from me
        Your love has surely died

I place my hand upon my heart
While tears trail down my face
You don't look back, you don't slow down
Instead, you quicken your pace

        True love cares, true love waits
        It does not walk away
        I plead silently with all my heart
        Just turn around and make my day

You don't look back, not even once –
You disappear from my sight
Now there's nothing, just my pain
Holding me close, holding me tight

        Loneliness is a hurting feeling
        I wish I could explain
        It comes at you from nowhere
        Enshrouding you in pain.

No one journeys through life unscathed –

— D.G. TORRENS

Fear Within

You stoked my fears
Seeding doubt within me

        I tell myself I am strong
          I will not submit

                Pain knows not from right or wrong
                          But you do

        I tell myself I am strong
          I will not submit

You are my weakness
You are my worst fear

        Pain knows not from right or wrong
          But you do.

Sent to Hell

You placed me on a mountaintop
Showing me the world from heaven

        Nothing could ever compare to this
          For you was my everything

                You gifted me a perfect world
                    The precipice was mine

        You worshipped me every day
      Then shot an arrow through my heart

You left me –
Fracturing my soul
And with that action

        You sent me straight to hell.

Buried Pain

I buried my pain
Beneath the ground

                It resurrected and sought me
                     Unexpectedly

                                  Like taunting ghosts
                                  Skulking in the shadows

          Seeking my weakness
          Searching for a way in

My armour weakened
Baring cracks

                And once again
                I fall into the abyss.

Gone From This World

I wait and wait for the longest time
I call out to you
Where are you?
Please find me
Don't leave me here
I miss you
I need you
I wait and wait for the longest time.

        I wait and wait for the longest time
        I call out to you
        I am shrouded in darkness alone and scared
        Where are you?
        My life has frozen
        All around me is still
        I wait and wait for the longest time.

                I wait and wait for the longest time
                I call out to you
                My heart is hurting
                My heart is crying
                Where are you?
                My life is cold without you
                I miss you so much
                I wait and wait for the longest time −

I wait and wait for the longest time
I call out to you

I wish I could touch you one last time
Living without you is just an existence
I miss you
Gone from this world
Abruptly taken
I wait and wait for the longest time.

Sorrow

Can you see sorrow in my eyes?
My inner pain is clear to see
I silence my cries, screaming inside
As memories of you flood my mind

>Can you see sorrow in my eyes?
>Grief has overwhelmed me
>I'm sorry, so very sorry
>It's too late now - the door has closed

Can you see sorrow in my eyes?
My pain has taken me hostage
A perpetual nightmare – it's real
I cannot let go –

>Can you see sorrow in my eyes?
>I should not have waited until after the event
>Can you see sorrow in my eyes?
>Please wait for me at God's eternal gates.

Inner Torment

They don't see me, not the real me
My tears are invisible, my pain hidden
I'm reaching out – my heart extended
They don't see me, not the real me

> A tear emerges – my tear ducts fill
> Not just tears - I'm drowning
> Can anyone see me and feel my pain?
> They don't see me, not the real me

What's the point of wings if you cannot fly?
My heart bears a burden – my heart is crying
I need to be heard – I trip over deaf ears
They don't see me, not the real me –

> If I have a guardian angel – please come to me now
> Wipe the tears from my face
> Remove the pain from my heart
> Make them hear and make them see
> As no one sees me, not the real me.

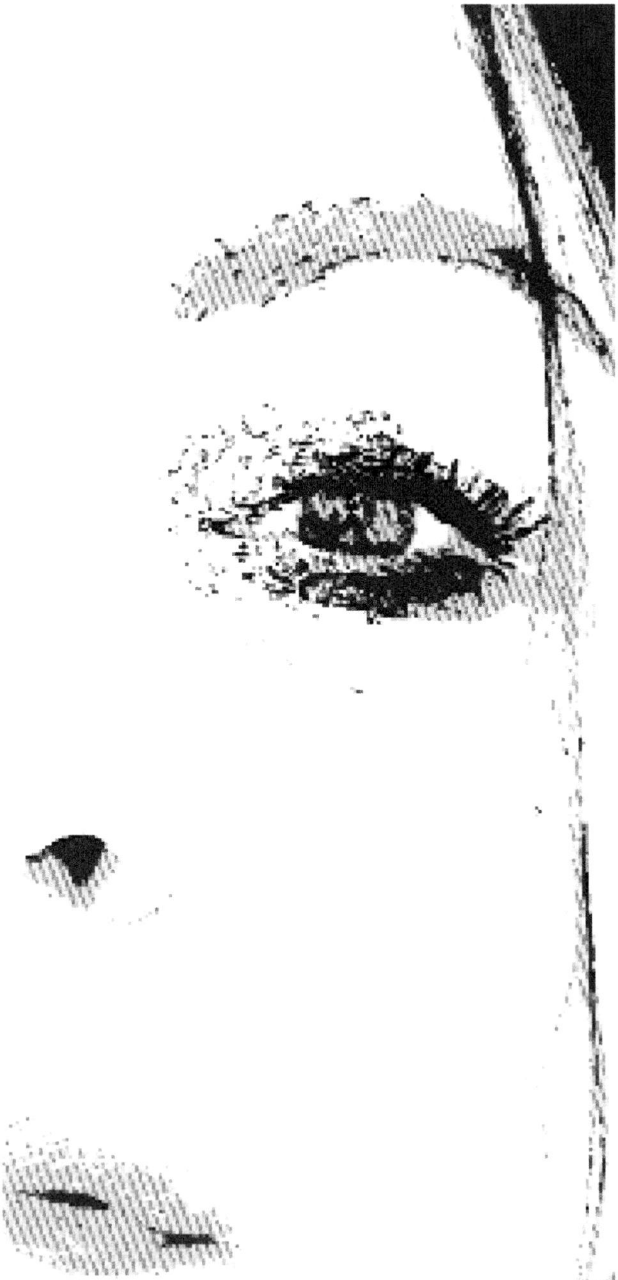

When white noise deafens you
leave the room –

D.G. Torrens

A Child's Desperate Plea

At 9 years old
SILENCED
Children should be seen and not heard
Afraid
'Don't interrupt me, go away'
At the brink
'Oh for goodness sake, what now?'
Her inner voice speaks
They don't care
I am in the way
SILENCED
At 13 years old
They see me now
The machines beeping around her
Looking down she sees her body
Panic ensues all around her
She feels light
Her pain has gone
Then the pull
She's back
She's alive
'They hear me now,' she whispers.

Childhood Trauma

I matured with pain
And buckets of tears
With each step taken
Over the years

My tears are memories
You cannot see
Trailing my cheeks
Knowing nothing is free

The pain I carry
Deep in my heart
Was delivered to me
From the very start

My trauma responses
Remind me each day
The neglect of a child
Never goes away.

I Wish I Could Factory Reset Our Planet

I wish I could factory reset our planet
To protect our children from the predators that roam it
So their innocence
Is not under constant threat
From the prey in the shadows
With their invisible net
A world where all children
Play with their friends
Without fear of nearby villains
No longer in corners
No longer afraid
Of the very people
By whom they're enslaved
I wish I could factory reset our
Planet
To rid the world of evil
That's constantly plaguing it.

A child's voice should

always be heard –

— D.G. TORRENS

Chapter Two

FIGHTING THE ABYSS

Shackled

Shackled and bound
I make to stand
Broken and cracked
I pause
Inhale, exhale
Rinse and repeat

> Shackled and bound
> I make to stand
> One step forward
> Dragging my chains
> Inhale, exhale
> Rinse and repeat

Shackled and bound
Determined to fight
Two steps forward
Three steps forward
I do not pause Inhale, exhale
Rinse and repeat –

> Shackled and bound
> I'm winning the fight
> I break my chains, I do not pause
> Heart pounding, feet running
> I broke my chains and won my fight.

Finding Me

I want to clean my soul
Free of you

                    And flood my veins
                    With freedom

                                      I want to remove the cling film
                                            Crushing my heart

My armour needs rebuilding
And my eyes need new sight

                    I'm ready to release you
                    And seek another me

                                                For I lost myself
                                            Deep in you

                Your moral compass floored
                Allowing me to journey blind
                Through a misguided sense of you.

Depression – I See You Now

You seed doubt in my mind
And take unconscious root
You lead me to my abyss
I descend
Swallowed up by the roots of your seed
Until
I awaken
I ascend

I SEE YOU NOW
You are the dark shadow lurking in the far corners of my mind
You prey on my weakness
But my will is strong
I SEE YOU NOW
The darkness that casts a web on my emotions
The darkness that lures me into your shadow

I SEE YOU NOW –
For I am strong
You are the darkness that preys on the vulnerable
The darkness that can envelope us all
I SEE YOU NOW
For I am strong
I pull out the roots and allow the light to flood through my mind
I SEE YOU NOW.

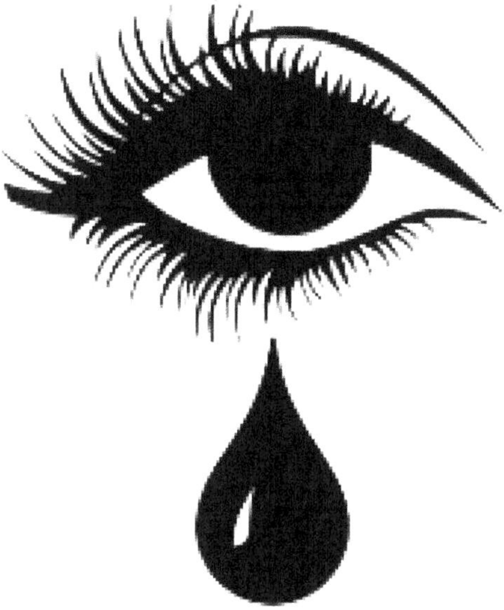

Chains were made to shackle but shackles can be broken –

— D.G. TORRENS

If Only

I wander passionately through
The mist of life
I form my own fantastical view
A view, I imagine the world should be

        No pain
        No suffering
        No war
        A fantastical view

                A dream
                One not realised during my lifetime
                A deep sadness envelopes me
                While that thought takes root

        IF ONLY
Even for just one day
There was no pain
        No suffering
        No war
My own fantastical view.

Labyrinth

Deep inside I'm lost
I cannot find my way back
I see a glimmer of light in the distance
I stand
I move forward
Yet I am still –
A labyrinth
Fraught with obstacles
I'm too tired to challenge

                    A labyrinth
          Once I would have navigated with ease
              I see the glimmer up ahead
                 I climb to my feet
                    Focus I say
                 Do not lose sight
           There is darkness at every turn
              My heart weighed down

                                  I stumble
                Then I remember, someone once said
                  'A star needs darkness to shine'
                         I rise to my feet
                My heart a little lighter now –
I am the star that needs the darkness to shine
                        My glow intensifies
                   And I am strong again.

I'm good today

I may not be tomorrow –

I'm sad today

I may not be tomorrow –

— D.G. TORRENS

Overcrowded Room

The need to escape an overcrowded room
Filled with a fog of people
Lots of talking – no listening
Fixed, fake smiles
I am suffocating
Drowning in a perpetual abyss
Screaming inside
I need to feel the cold breeze on my face
Something
Anything
As long as it's real
I step outside
The cold night air envelops me
I smile
I inhale
I feel it
It's real
I am alone, yet comforted
I leave the fog of people behind
I ascend from the abyss
I am free.

Clarity is often found amidst the silence –

— D.G. TORRENS

Hidden Light

There is light we can see and light we can't see
You are the light that I cannot see
Invisible but there
Light hiding in the darkness
Making the unbearable bearable
Enveloping the shadows in my mind
Protecting me from my doubts
You are the invisible light
That promotes a better me Encouraging me to shine
When my light is all but a flicker
From inside of me you shine
Casting your illuminating glow
A glow that enables me to –
Put one foot in front of the other
You are my determined self –
A fighter with conviction
You fight the darkness within and enable me to shine.

Would You Break My Fall?

If I were freefalling, would you break my fall?
Enveloping me mid-flight
My instinct tells me you would turn away
The truth of you fractures my tormented heart
A heart you stole without thought
My heart a willing hostage
The truth of you eluded me I see you now
If I were free falling
I would not extend my hand
I would spread my wings and ascend
For I know I am stronger without you.

Absent

You are here
But always absent

                Your physical presence
                    Is not enough

                                  If your heart and soul
                                      Have taken leave

                What is it you seek?
                For I know not me.

Memories Manifest into Tears

Sometimes, my memories manifest into tears
Trailing down my cheeks
Sometimes, the pain of my memories replaces the blood
Flowing through my veins
I lock the door of my memory bank
But those banked memories ooze out liquid pictures
Taunting me
Disabling me
Like an enemy trying to imprison me
I search deep into the depths of my mind
There I find a moment
I smile
No longer afraid
I regain my strength –
I rise from the floor
No longer disabled
No longer taunted
For I am strong.

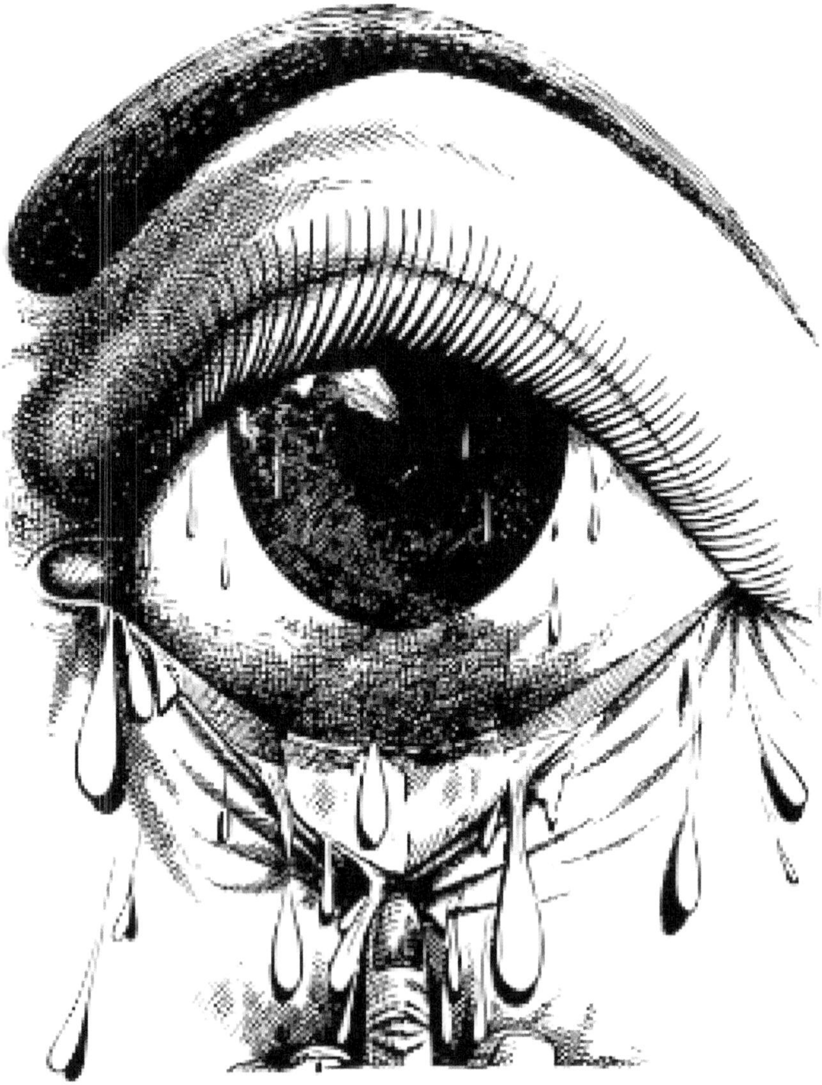

Your Painful Gifts

I gifted you my trust
You gifted me deceit

        I gifted you my heart
        You gifted me lies

                I gifted you hope
                You gifted me pain

        I gift you no more
        You gift me your leave

When I stopped giving to you
My heart gifted me peace.

Shards of My Heart

Shards of my heart scattered
Time will not heal

        Time is merely a bridge we cross
        A bridge that makes pain bearable

                Time does not heal the broken
                The broken become strong

        Crossing the bridge of time
        A bridge designed to lessen the hurt

Time comforts the broken and lessens the pain
But our hearts will always remember.

We often emerge stronger

from our darkest moments –

— D.G. TORRENS

The Enemy Within

The sun emerges
Drinking up the rain in my life

        The clouds have receded
        Exposing the light

                The corners of my mouth turn up
                  Revealing a long-awaited smile

        My reluctant friend –
        Hiding in the shadows of my mind
        Gone for now

I bask in the sun while I can
For I know my nemesis will return.

My Wings Are Broken

My wings are broken
I am free falling
No cushion in sight

                No one to break my fall
          The wind wraps around me – the only thing

                        between me and the approaching ground
                              Darkness envelopes me like a
                                    Reluctant friend

                I do not accept my fate
                I do not hit the ground
                    I swoop
                    I rise

My wings maybe broken
But my spirit lives on.

Memories Are Long

Memories are long when they are bad
Unforgettable fragments -
Hiding in the shadows of your mind
Making unwanted appearances -
Refusing to leave
Memories are long when they hurt
The pain of them keeps us moving
Instilling conviction for all that we do
Those memories –
That steal space in the corners of your mind,
Dark shadows following you everywhere you go,
You cannot erase them
But you can defeat the hold they have on you.

White Noise

I hear nothing in this loud overbearing room

        Nothing but white noise
        So many people filled with
        Empty words

                My eyes fill in the gaps
            My eyes make sense of the chaos before me

    Judgements are made without knowledge
    Decisions are made without reason

People cast aside without thought
I hear nothing in this loud overbearing room
But my eyes see all and gain much wisdom.

Time Does Not Heal The Broken

Time does not heal that which is broken
Time merely acts as a bridge

    Allowing you to cross without falling
    A pained heart does not forget

        It reminds you when you are most vulnerable
            When your soul is in despair

    And hope has taken leave
Your weakest moment becomes your strongest.

A Burdened Heart

Your presence burdens my heart
For I cannot have you

        Yet you confuse me with your eyes
        Those eyes that penetrate deeply

                Piercing the core of my soul –
                  I turn away to no avail

        I feel your eyes lasering me
        Yet I cannot have you

I do the only sane thing I can do – I walk away.

Days I Miss

        Some days I'm shrouded in darkness
           No light is coming through
           I can't explain my feelings
            Only you can help you

There are no words for my abyss
No one would understand
So many days I find I miss
I reject all helping hands

        I can be strong – I will reach high
         My nemesis won't keep me long
       I fight the darkness and open my eyes
        To find the light that's shining strong

My inner strength will see me through
The darkness has now passed
Once again, I fought my abyss
I can smile again at last.

Broken Soldier

One less limb, home he returns
Once a soldier, much he learned

      Death is a fact, just not how
      Redundant and wandering he is now

            Fighting his way through every day
            Searching for answers along the way

Alone with his fears, he now feels
While waiting for his broken body to heal

      He will not beaten, he will survive
      He made it home, he's still alive

            One less limb and homebound now
            Fear still lurking, he battles somehow.

There will always be those who delight in weaponising your weaknesses

be mindful who you share your secrets with –

— D.G. TORRENS

You Ascended

You never said goodbye
That coffee never materialised
GONE –
Just like that
Leaving a gaping hole in my chest
You ascended to another place
A place I cannot reach you
I want that coffee
I want to see you
You are gone
Gone for always
Sadness envelopes my entire being
I miss you
Just one last coffee
Or even a goodbye –
I see you in my dreams
Then my eyes open –
It's real
GONE -
You are really gone
Tragically swept away forever
I will see you in my dreams
Gone from this world maybe
But always in my dreams.

The One

A tsunami of emotions
Tearing through my mind
Fragmented memories hover in the shadows
You were the one – the only one
My beating heart pounds through my chest
Resurfaced memories haunting me
Reminding me that once – I was loved irrevocably
Thoughts of us intoxicate all that I am
Emerging from the shadows of my mind – all of you
No longer fragments
I remember us
And all that we were
You're gone
You ascended to a higher plane
You will always be my one.

Deafening Silence

I walk through the door to a deafening silence
My eyes dart from room to room
Then I remember –
And fall to my knees
You are gone
You are no longer here
I release a piercing scream
I clamp my mouth, quelling my cries
You are gone –
You are really gone.

The Only Truth of War-Suffering

Coffins will pile up graves will be many
Mouring will be widespread for soldiers aplenty
The skies will blacken with the ashes of the dead
Reminiscent of WWII every one of us dread

A nuclear option is crystal clear
While an apocalyptic storm looms near
Unstable dictators with no fear of death
Hold the power to steal our very last breath

False pretexts instils fear for all on the ground
Dictators and leaders showcase weapons all around
Nothing will be gained from this continued insanity
Only unconscionable suffering for the whole of humanity.

Domestic Violence-in Childhood

I experienced great pain in my youth
Sadly under my own roof
Locked in my room
Weapons of choice
Studded belts and wooden brooms

Living daily with parental
hate crimes
Those are my memories
From childhood times

Torn apart from my siblings
Thrown in to state care
All in different places
Alone and scared

Only to realise
This was no safe haven
The neglect continued
By the institution's patron

I am an adult now
And learned to survive
A success I have made
But there's pain in my eyes.

Chapter Three

BEYOND THE ABYSS

Following the Crowd

Following the crowd
Will not
Always lead
You to
Your
Destination –
Sometimes
You need
To break away
And change
Direction
To get to where
You want
To be –

When I feel down

I remind myself that I gave life to another

human being

and that is pretty miraculous –

— D.G. TORRENS

Hidden In The Silence

You can find me
In the silence
In a room filled with chaos

        Look past the lips that spill
        And the judgmental eyes

                Walk past the ignorant
                And skirt past the bigoted

      I am the observer
      Taking leave of the crowd
      Seeing what cannot be seen.

Not Defective - Just Human

A demon has many heads
Which one are you?
'Hi my name is grief'
What is yours?
Depression
Loneliness
Sorrow
I recognise that look in your eyes
It's ok
We are not defective
We are human
Take my hand
Let's walk together
And share our inner battles.

I do not need to hear excuses

Your actions have provided all the truth I need–

— D.G. TORRENS

Peace In Solitude

I feel the peace of my own solitude

        I am not alone for I am with me
        Enveloped in perpetual calmness – a beauty unseen

                I revel in my quietness
                Shrouded in pure silence

    Yet I hear the whispers of the world around me
    The sublimity of my solitude bears me new sight

The intellectual sight to see what should always be seen.

The Seasons Of Abyss

A periodic visit

                        Inevitable

                                            Like the seasons

                Each visit is different

Yet familiar.

                I'm no longer afraid

                                For I know the seasons change.

Ignorance and Bigotry

We are not separated by colour, race or religion

    We are separated by blindness, ignorance and bigotry
        Of our own making

                In order to see the person
                You must first open your eyes
                And clear out the dirt

    Cut a vein and we all bleed red.

With the courage of conviction I battle

over mountains even if it means I walk alone –

— D.G. TORRENS

A Writer's Mind

Remnants of a writer's mind

      Whispered words floating in the wind

            Releasing fragments of inner truths

      Revealing a perpetually tortured soul

A brief encounter A candid view

      The remnants of a writer's mind.

Far Beneath the Deep

Submerged beneath the surface
Enshrouded by a shoal of fish
Beauty at its purest
As nature intended

        Beneath the deep
        Another world
        Untouched by human hands
        BUT FOR HOW LONG –

        Can it evade contamination? –

The human hand –
Nature's worst enemy
I extend my arm
Immerse myself in untouched perfection.
Nature's perfection –
Far beneath the deep.

Before The Fight is Lost

A blackened cloud looms over us all

            We cannot close our eyes
           We cannot turn away

                      We are all affected by imminent rainfall
                            Soon to be unleashed

      The world is broken and the wounds are expanding

We need to unite and fight for humanity –
Before the fight is lost to us all.

Life emerges from the tears of our skies feeding the land So we can flourish -

— D.G. TORRENS

I See the Bigger Picture

I see the bigger picture
A picture that eludes the masses
I am not blind for I truly see
I see humanity's self-destruction
Our world is at the mercy of humankind
Once it was perfect
Untouched
Plenished with all that we needed
But then came the walls
Divided lands
Led only by greed for more
What more did we really need
When all we needed, we had
I see the bigger picture
For I am not blind
We are losing
The biggest loss of all –
Our once plentiful land.

I crash to the floor following another life fall –

'Stand up'

I tell myself the floor is no place for you.

— D.G. TORRENS

Fight or Flight

I choose to fight
I will not recoil
You cannot have me today
My will is strong
I choose to fight
You cannot have me today
My abyss disappears
I inhale a deep breath
My will was strong today.

You Found Me

In the depths of despair
When all seemed lost
You appeared before me
Like an apparition
Life was throwing me a helping hand
For this, I'm forever grateful

>In the depths of despair
>When I could fall no lower
>You stood before me
>With a guiding light
>For this, I'm forever grateful

In the depths of despair
When all seemed lost
And I'd lost the will to live
You opened your heart
You let me in
For this, I'm forever grateful

>In the depths of despair
>When all seemed lost
>A new friendship was born
>My vision of life changed that day
>For this, I'm forever grateful.

A Challenge From God

You challenged my soul
You challenged my spirit
I accepted my fate
I did not fear it
You tested my strength
And inner wrath
This did not deter me
From my chosen path

When I was brutally close to defeat
I remained true to my heart
My every beat
My destiny would one day
Be in my control
Regardless of obstacles I was once told –

I believe I have passed
Your arduous test
And deserve to live my life
How it suits me best
Why you chose me
I will never know
But your onerous test
Has helped me to grow
It took a long time
For me to understand
That the challenge you set me
Was a helping hand.

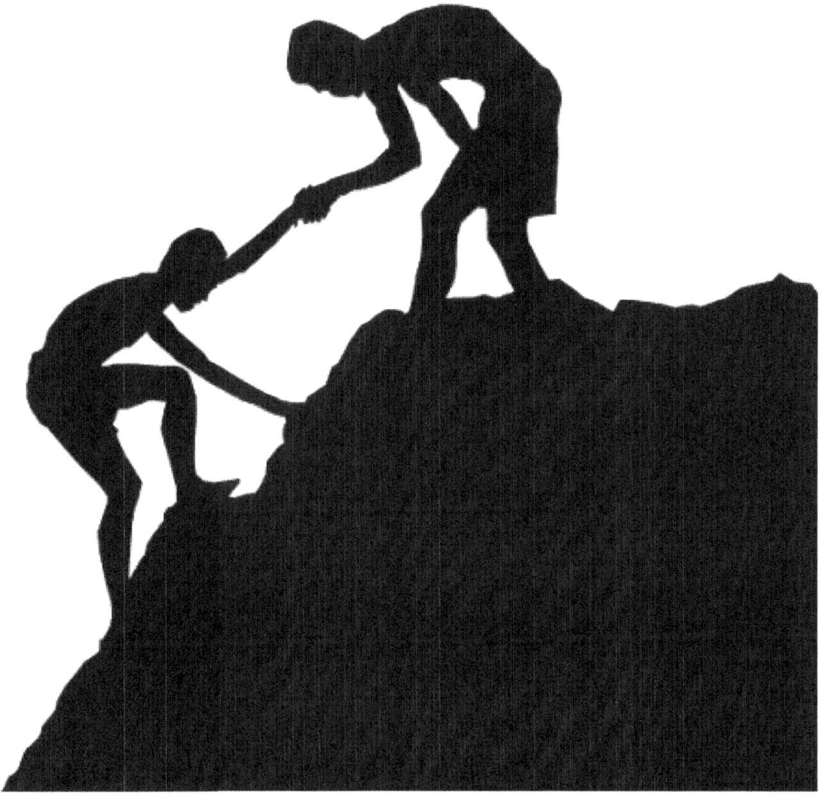

Kindness is a suture for the broken–

— D.G. TORRENS

Collective Thought

A world in deep need of repair
Filled with humans suffering despair
An imminent storm circles our lands
The signs are clear but we misunderstand
The oceans spill and the fires rage
Our lands are rumbling
Are we disengaged?
Eyes wide shut and ears closed
While an apocalyptic cloud lurks unopposed
Disguised as saviours leading us blind
To the detriment of humankind
Maybe our hope is collective thought

To breathe new life on what humans wrought.

— D.G. TORRENS

A Murder of Crows

A MURDER OF CROWS
Perched in a tree
Loud and rambunctious
People fear thee
Urban legends
Sweep our minds
But social and caring
You will find
A MURDER OF CROWS
Perched in a tree
Should not be feared
As per history
Wise and clever
Surveying their space
Picking you out
They'll recognise your face
A MURDER OF CROWS
Are not a threat
A murder of dictators
Now that I would bet
When did you hear
That crows did kill
A story I'm guessing
Told to chill.

Feed Your Heart

A heart needs to flourish

        Like a seedling needs water

To break through the soil

        And bask in the light.

Our Beautiful Scars

For each emotional scar we bare
Reminds us we survived

    We're equipped to journey with pain
    And weather the storms before us
    Our scars are an important reminder

        That our strength is deep within
          That we are strong

    We won the fight
    And battled through the pain.

Negative Influences

Negative influences devour the spirit
Intoxicating your soul

        Enveloping you in a perpetual darkness
        Step away

            Don't allow them to feast on your emotions
                Free yourself and let go

        Make your journey with conviction
        You have a destination in mind
        A Dream
        A Goal

This is your life no one else's
Live it your way, not theirs –

Soar like an eagle
Spread your wings
And ascend.

Journey With Conviction

We search to find us Between each step
We're lost
Direction evades us
Clarity eludes us
We stop
We remain still
We close our eyes
And breathe
Then breathe some more
A smile emerges
Our path is clear to us now
Keep stepping forward
Avoid all junctions
Walk straight and do not be deterred
For our destiny is waiting at the end of our journey.

One Simple Word

A random word interrupts my thoughts
Persistent and overtaking my mind
I pause
I digest
My thoughts now corrupted
My data lost
But for this one word
Determined to make a point I close my eyes
Allowing silence to envelope me
One word
One simple word
A word that changed the course of my day –
PEACE.

Glowing Embers

The glowing embers of my dream
Still burning

            Refusing to die out
         A perpetual glow that remains strong

                        They cannot be blown away
                        They cannot be washed away

           Their resolve is strong
            My dream cannot die

Let the clouds unleash its contents
For my embers will always glow.

Reminiscing

Looking back reminiscing over what used to be
A bewildering journey, was that really me
It seems so long ago, a different girl, a different life
When life was an obstacle and my path plagued by strife
I look to my child and cannot believe
I made it this far, so much I've achieved
With the strength of will and strength of mind
My place in life, I eventually find
Looking back, reminiscing over all my struggles
When life was full of woes and troubles
It seems so long ago, a different girl, a different life
When life was an obstacle and my path plagued by strife.

I looked into the eye of my abyss

I said

NO –

not today

my mind is not available for your pleasure –

— D.G. TORRENS

Note From the Author

Everyone's journey through life is unique
We all suffer emotionally at some point
We all find ourselves in a dark place
It is an inevitable part of living –
It's not defective – it's human.

About The Author

D.G. Torrens is an international bestselling author. D.G is also a founding member of bestsellingreads.com and Author City UK. D.G is also a co-owner of Contrary Trees Film Productions and is currently producing a documentary film in Birmingham UK due for release late autumn 2024.

You can find the author on Twitter: @Torrenstp
Website: dgtorrensauthor.com

Printed in Great Britain
by Amazon